Celebrating Grown Ups Day

Written by Krista Tarasyuk

Some children live with just moms.

Some children live with just dads.

Some children are living with their grandparents.

Some children are living with their aunts or uncles.

Some children are living with
foster parents.

Some children are living with older
siblings.

Some children have a mom and a dad.

We should have a day that we can celebrate all of them together!

We all have grown ups in our lives.
They deserve to have a day.

We can make them a hand made card.
We can dance the day away.

We can do something special.
We can do something new.

We can even sing them a new
song we wrote, or two.

Our grown ups are so special
Because even though they're
different…

They support us every day.
They are so significant;

Making yummy dinners..
Washing all our stinky clothes..

Making sure we brush our teeth..
Wiping off our snotty nose..

Making sure we look both ways
Before we cross the street..

Making sure we sit
And be still when we eat.

Making sure our shoelaces each
have a double knot..

Picking us up from school when
our forehead is too hot..

Helping us with our homework
and helping us read..

Helping us learn and understand
so we succeed..

Wiping off our dirty hands
Or wiping away tears..

Allowing us to climb in their bed
When the night triggers fears.

We would be lost without them
and we want them all to know
that even though we are little,
like us, our love continues to
grow!

www.ingramcontent.com/pod-product-compliance
Lightning Source LLC
Chambersburg PA
CBHW020948160726

47993CB00007B/2994